AF264855

REMARKS ON STRONGLY ELLIPTIC PARTIAL
DIFFERENTIAL EQUATIONS

by Louis Nirenberg

1. Introduction

In recent years the interest in extending the theory of
boundary value problems of second order elliptic equations to
equations of higher order and to systems has grown considerably.
The Dirichlet problem for such equations has been investigated
by M. I. Vishik [26], F. E. Browder [1] and L. Gårding [11],
see also K. O. Friedrichs [10] and C. B. Morrey [20]. The
methods used for a single equation extend to the Dirichlet
problem for an elliptic system in N functions $u_1,\ldots,u_N$ which
is of the same order in all functions, and which is strongly
elliptic in the sense defined by Vishik [26]. Other boundary
value problems have been considered by Browder [2] and Jacques-
Louis Lions [19].

The successful treatment of the general equation has been
based on some form of the projection theorem in Hilbert space,
as employed for example by H. Weyl in [27]. The method is, of
course, related to the classical variational method, the
Dirichlet principle, which has been of extensive use in treating
elliptic equations, see for instance Courant-Hilbert [5]. The
applicability of the method is based on a single inequality
expressing the positive definiteness of the Dirichlet integral
associated with the differential operator. This inequality
furnishes bounds on the square integrals of derivatives of
solutions. For general equations with variable coefficients
this inequality is due to L. Gårding [11], and extends
immediately to Vishik's strongly elliptic systems. For second
order systems with constant coefficients the inequality was
derived earlier by L. Van Hove [25].

For the elliptic equation

$$Lu = f$$

in a domain $\mathcal{D}$, (for which Gårding's inequality has been
established), the projection method leads easily to the
construction of a function u having derivatives in some
generalized sense, and which is a weak solution of the equation,
i.e. which satisfies

$$(L^{*}\phi, u) = (\phi, f)$$

for all infinitely differentiable functions ϕ with compact
support in the domain. Here L^{*} is the formal adjoint of L and
$(\ ,\ )$ denotes the L_2 scalar product. Having constructed a
weak solution u it then becomes necessary to prove the
differentiability of u in the classical sense. If in addition
u is a generalized solution of a boundary value problem, it is
also necessary to show that certain derivatives of u are
continuous in the closure of the domain and satisfy the
prescribed boundary data. The first problem, that of
differentiability in the interior of $\mathcal{D}$ has been treated by a
number of authors using different techniques. F. John [15]
has proved the differentiability for very general equations
using his method of spherical means. Another approach is based
on the use of the fundamental solution of the equation, the
existence of which has been established by F. John [14]. This
has been employed by L. Schwartz [23] and Browder [1(a)].
There is a third method which is consistent with the Hilbert
space approach to the existence theory and operates merely
with estimates for the square integrals of derivatives of a
solution. This approach, which is based solely on Gårding's
inequality, and is therefore restricted to strongly elliptic
systems, has been carried out by Friedrichs [10] and also by
Browder [1(c)].

The problem of establishing smoothness of the solution up
to the boundary, and the assumption of boundary data, has
remained open for some time, even for equations with constant
coefficients. For equations of second order this problem has
recently been solved by C. B. Morrey [20], who has given a very

extensive treatment of second order elliptic systems. The case
of a single second order equation in the plane is already
contained in Courant-Hilbert [5] pp. 495.

In this paper we prove by elementary means that the
generalized solution has the required smoothness properties up
to the boundary and is therefore a solution of the boundary
value problem in the classical sense. We also indicate how the
concept of strong ellipticity can be extended to systems of
equations which are not of the same order in the unknown
functions.

The whole Hilbert space theory of the Dirichlet problem,
including the identification of the generalized solution with
the classical one, can be based on the single Gårding inequality,
and we shall give a complete discussion of the problem from
this point of view.

For simplicity we treat the case of a single equation
$Lu = f$, for $u(x)$, $x = (x_1,\ldots,x_u)$ in a bounded domain Ω, and
describe later the extension to our strongly elliptic systems.

Using D to denote differentiation $D : (D_{x_1},\ldots,D_{x_n})$, and
$D^i u$ to denote any derivative of u of order j we consider the
equation with complex coefficients of order m in the form

$$(1.1) \qquad Lu \equiv \sum_{\rho,\sigma=0}^{m} (-1)^{\rho} D^{\rho} a^{\rho,\sigma} D^{\sigma} u = f \quad ,$$

where summation is first extended over all derivatives D^{ρ}, D^{σ}
of orders ρ and σ. The operator is elliptic if for every real
vector $\xi : (\xi_1,\ldots,\xi_n)$ the characteristic form $\xi^m a^{m,m} \xi^m$ (where
there is clearly a summation implied) is different from zero
when $\xi \neq 0$.

In §3 we solve the Dirichlet problem for (1.1) using a
modification of the projection theorem - a generalized
representation for bounded linear functionals, due to P. D. Lax
and A. Milgram [18], which enables one to treat at once non-
symmetric elliptic operators. In §2 we introduce the well
known Friedrichs and Sobolev classes of functions [8, 24] having
generalized derivatives. Some aspects of their calculus is
studied; in particular, we call attention to the useful Lemmas

The new material is contained in §§4-6.

In §4 we give a self-contained proof of the differentiability of weak solutions of (1.1), which is a simplification of that of Friedrichs [10]. The proof proceeds by differencing the equation and applying Gårding's inequality to derive estimates for the difference quotients of the solution. A similar approach has independently been devised by Paul Berg. In another paper in this issue P. D. Lax [17] has presented an elegant discussion of the whole question of differentiability of solutions of partial differential equations, and has also given a proof in the Hilbert space framework of the differentiability of weak solutions. In §5 we prove the classical assumption of boundary values in a smoothly bounded domain; the proof is based on the elementary Lemma 6 of §2. Browder has recently discovered another proof which employs an inequality of N. Aronszajn in place of Lemma 6 of §2, and requires weaker conditions of the function f.

Strongly elliptic systems are introduced in §6. These are a subclass of the very general elliptic systems studied by A. Douglis and L. Nirenberg in another paper [6] in this issue. As an illustration we present an example involving functions $u(x,y)$, $v(x,y)$:

$$(1.2) \quad \begin{aligned} (D_x^2 + D_y^2)u - D_y^4 v + L_{11}u + L_{12}v &= f_1 \ , \\ D_y^4 u + (D_x^2 + D_y^2)^3 v + L_{21}u + L_{22}v &= f_2 \ , \end{aligned}$$

where L_{11}, L_{12}, L_{21}, L_{22} are arbitrary linear differential operators of 1-st, 3-rd, 3-rd and 5-th order, respectively. As shown in §6, the following is a well posed Dirichlet problem for this system: prescribe the values of

$$u \ , \quad v \ , \quad \frac{\partial v}{\partial n}, \quad \frac{\partial^2 v}{\partial n^2} \ ,$$

on the boundary (where $\partial/\partial n$ denotes differentiation in the normal direction) - this despite the fact that fourth order derivatives of u occur in the system.

Since the whole discussion given here is based on the single Gårding inequality, (3.6), with other known estimates ignored, our differentiability theorems are not proved under the weakest possible conditions on the coefficients of the equations, such as in Morrey [20]. Combining the results obtained here with the differentiability theorems in §8 of Douglis, Nirenberg [6] one clearly obtains much stronger differentiability statements. The author, in a paper under preparation, has obtained strong differentiability theorems for general systems, analogous to those of Morrey [20] for systems of second order, with the aid of results by A. P. Calderon and A. Zygmund [4].

2. Function Spaces and Their Calculus

We consider a fixed bounded domain $\mathcal{D}$ (open point set) in n-space with boundary $\dot{\mathcal{D}}$ and closure $\bar{\mathcal{D}}$.

Definition. $\mathcal{D}$ is of class C_j, for integral $j \geq 1$, provided there exists a finite number of subdomains, called patches, which together with a compact subdomain of $\mathcal{D}$ cover $\bar{\mathcal{D}}$, such that the closure $\bar{\mathcal{U}}$ of each patch $\mathcal{U}$ may be mapped in a one-to-one way onto a closed domain, with $\dot{\mathcal{D}} \cap \mathcal{U}$ mapped onto a set lying in an n-1 dimensional plane, and such that the mapping and inverse mapping are j times continuously differentiable.

Unless the contrary is stated the letter ϕ will always be used to represent test functions: infinitely differentiable functions with compact support in $\mathcal{D}$, i.e. vanishing near $\dot{\mathcal{D}}$.

We introduce in a well known manner certain function spaces which are Hilbert spaces and summarize briefly some of their properties. For complex valued functions u having continuous derivatives up to order $j \geq 0$ in $\mathcal{D}$ define the norm

$$(2.1) \qquad |u|_j^2 = \sum_{i=0}^{j} \int |D^i u|^2 dx$$

and the associated scalar product

$$(u,v)_j = \sum_{i=0}^{j} \int D^i u \overline{D^i v} \, dx \ .$$

In such sums it will always be understood that summation
extends first over all derivatives of the orders shown. All
integrations will extend over $\mathcal{D}$. We define the following
Hilbert spaces (Friedrichs [8], Sobolev [24]):

H_j: The completion of the set of such functions with respect
to the norm $| \ |_j$.

$\mathring{H}_j$: The closure of the subspace of H_j spanned by test
functions. The associated norms and spaces relative to a sub-
domain $\mathcal{A}$ will be denoted by $| \ |_j^{\mathcal{A}}$, $H_j^{\mathcal{A}}$, $\mathring{H}_j^{\mathcal{A}}$. Clearly a function
in H_j is also in L_2. The spaces H_0, $\mathring{H}_0$ are simply the L_2
spaces in $\mathcal{D}$ and we use (u,v) to denote the scalar product in
this space.

A function is said to have strong derivatives up to order
j in a domain if it belongs to $H_j^{\mathcal{A}}$ for every compact subdomain $\mathcal{A}$.
In $\mathcal{A}$ we then have a sequence of approximating functions $\{u_n\}$
with $|u_n - u|_j^{\mathcal{A}} \to 0$. The limits in H_0 of their derivatives
$D^i u_n$, $i \le j$, are called strong derivatives $D^i u$ of u in $\mathcal{A}$.
To see that these are uniquely defined we introduce the concept
of weak derivative. A function u in $\mathcal{D}$ is said to have a weak
derivative $D^j u = v$ if u and v are functions in $H_0^{\mathcal{A}}$ in every
compact subdomain $\mathcal{A}$ and if for every test function ϕ the
identity

$$(2.2) \qquad \int u D^j \phi \, dx = (-1)^j \int v \phi \, dx$$

holds. It follows immediately from (2.2) that weak derivatives
are uniquely defined. In addition it is easily seen that
strong derivatives in $\mathcal{A}$ are also weak derivatives in $\mathcal{A}$; they
are therefore also uniquely defined in $\mathcal{A}$. It follows that
they are well defined functions in $\mathcal{D}$ belonging to $H_0^{\mathcal{A}}$ in every
compact subdomain $\mathcal{A}$. We observe also that the natural em-
bedding of H_j in H_0 is one-to-one.

Now for a few remarks on the calculus of strong derivatives the proofs of which are merely sketched and left to the
reader.

First of all it is easily seen that a function in H_j remains in H_j under a continuous one-to-one change of independent variable which, together with the inverse transformation, has continuous bounded derivatives up to order j, and that the standard chain rule formulas for differentiation hold.

We also observe that the usual identities for integration by parts hold for functions having strong derivatives provided both sides of the identities are meaningful for these functions.

Lemma 1. If a function u belongs to L_2 in D and is the weak (in L_2) limit of a sequence of functions u_n in H_j with uniformly bounded norms $|u_n|_j$ then u belongs to H_j and its derivatives up to order j are the weak limits of the corresponding derivatives of the functions u_n.

Proof: By choosing a subsequence if necessary we may suppose that all derivatives of the u_n up to order j converge weakly. The result for the subsequence then follows by repeated application of a theorem of Banach-Saks which asserts that a weakly convergent sequence in Hilbert space has a subsequence whose arithmetic means converge strongly to the weak limit.[2] Since the derivatives of u are uniquely defined it then follows that they are the weak limits of the derivatives of the original sequence, not merely the subsequence.

Lemma 2. If u is strongly differentiable up to order i and the i-th order derivatives of u are strongly differentiable up to order j then u is strongly differentiable up to order $i+j$.

This is most easily proved with the aid of the Friedrichs mollifiers [9] which we describe briefly. Let $j(x)$ be an infinitely differentiable function in n-space with support in the unit sphere $|x| < 1$ and suppose $j(x) \geq 0$, and

$$\int j(x)dx = 1 .$$

In any subdomain Ω of D whose distance to $\dot{D}$ is greater than ε the smoothing operator, or mollifier, is defined as

---

[2] A simple proof is given in Riesz-Nagy [21], §38.

$$(2.3) \qquad J_\varepsilon u = \varepsilon^{-n} \int J(\tfrac{x-y}{\varepsilon}) u(y)\, dy \quad .$$

Clearly J_ε commutes with differentiation. In addition it has the following established properties.

$$(2.4) \qquad \begin{aligned} &\lim_{\varepsilon \to 0} |J_\varepsilon u - u|_0^a = 0 \; , \\[2mm] &|J_\varepsilon u|_0^a \leq |u|_0 \quad . \end{aligned}$$

To prove the lemma consider a subdomain a of $\mathcal{D}$ whose distance to $\dot{\mathcal{D}}$ is greater than some $\varepsilon_0 > 0$. We find easily that

$$\lim_{\varepsilon \to 0} |J_\varepsilon u - u|_0^a = 0$$

and that $|J_\varepsilon u|_{i+k}^a$ is bounded by a constant independent of ε for $\varepsilon < \frac{1}{2}\varepsilon_0$. The result follows by Lemma 1. (It can also be easily seen that in a the derivatives of $J_\varepsilon u$ up to order $i+j$ converge in the mean as $\varepsilon \to 0$.)

Lemma 3. Let $\mathcal{D}_1, \ldots, \mathcal{D}_k$ be subdomains of $\mathcal{D}$ with $\mathcal{D} \subset \cup \mathcal{D}_i$. Suppose a function u in $\mathcal{D}$ belongs to H_j for each $\mathcal{D}_i$ then u belongs to H_j in $\mathcal{D}$.

Proof: We sketch the proof only for $j = 1$; a similar argument holds for other j. Let $1 = \sum_1^N \phi_i$ be a partition of unity in $\mathcal{D}$ where the function ϕ_1 is infinitely differentiable and has the property that $\mathcal{D} \cap$ (the support of ϕ_i) is contained in one of the $\mathcal{D}_1, \ldots, \mathcal{D}_k$, say $\mathcal{D}_{\rho_i}$, $i = 1, \ldots, N$. Since, in $\mathcal{D}_\rho$, u belongs to H_1 there exists a sequence of differentiable functions $\{u_n^{(\rho)}\}$ in $\mathcal{D}_\rho$ converging in the mean to u, and with mean convergent first derivatives $Du_n^{(\rho)}$.

Construct the sequence of function in $\mathcal{D}$

$$u_n = \sum_i \phi_i u_n^{(\rho_i)} \quad .$$

From the equations

$$u_n - u = \sum_i \phi_i (u_n^{(\rho_i)} - u) \; ,$$

$$Du_n = \sum_i \phi_i Du_n^{(\rho_i)} + \sum_i (D\phi_i) \cdot (u_n^{(\rho_i)} - u)$$

it follows easily that u_n converges in the mean to u in $\mathcal{B}$ and that the first derivatives Du_n converge in the mean in $\mathcal{B}$ proving that u is in H_1.

Consequently strong differentiability is a purely local property.

Corollary. If to every point in $\mathcal{B}$ there is a neighborhood $\mathcal{A}$ in which u belongs to $H_j^{\mathcal{A}}$ then u is j times strongly differentiable in $\mathcal{B}$.

Lemma 4. Let $\mathcal{A}$ be a bounded domain whose boundary is made up of two disjoint point sets $\mathcal{A}_1$, $\mathcal{A}_2$ with $\mathcal{A}_1$ contained in some hyperplane, say $x_n = a$ const., c. If u is j times strongly differentiable in $\mathcal{A}$ and if its strong derivatives are in $H_0^{\mathcal{A}}$ then u belongs to $H_j^{\mathcal{B}}$ for any subdomain $\mathcal{B}$ of $\mathcal{A}$ which is bounded away from $\mathcal{A}_2$.

Note that the subdomain may touch $\mathcal{A}_1$.

Proof: Let $\mathcal{B}$ be a subdomain of $\mathcal{A}$ whose distance to $\mathcal{A}_1$ is at least $\varepsilon_0 > 0$. We may suppose that points in $\mathcal{B}$ near $\mathcal{A}_2$ have coordinate $x_n >$ the constant c. In $\mathcal{B}$ apply a modified mollifier to u,

$$(J_\varepsilon' u)(x) = \varepsilon^{-n} \int_{\mathcal{A}} j(\frac{x_\varepsilon - y}{\varepsilon}) u(y) dy \; , \qquad \varepsilon < \varepsilon_0 \; ,$$

where x_ε is related to $x = (x_1, \ldots, x_n)$ by

$$x_\varepsilon = (x_1, \ldots, x_n + \varepsilon) \; .$$

It is easily seen that $\lim\limits_{\varepsilon \to 0} |J_\varepsilon' u - u|_0^{\mathcal{B}} = 0$ and that $|J_\varepsilon' u|_j^{\mathcal{B}}$ is bounded by a constant independent of h. The result follows by Lemma 1. (It is in fact easily seen that the derivatives of $J_\varepsilon' u$ up to order j converge in the mean in $\mathcal{B}$).

By breaking up a smooth domain into an interior domain and boundary patches, applying Lemmas 3 and 4 we may easily derive

Lemma 5. <u>Let u be strongly differentiable up to order j in a domain $\mathcal{D}$ of class C_j. If its strong derivatives are in H_0 then u belongs to H_j.</u>

Lemma 6. <u>Let u belong to H_j, $j > 0$, in a domain $\mathcal{D}$ of class C_2. For sufficiently small $\varepsilon > 0$ there exists a constant $c(\varepsilon,j)$ depending only on ε and j such that</u>

$$(2.5) \qquad |u|^2_{j-1} \leq c|u|^2_j + c(\varepsilon,j)|u|^2_0 \ .$$

For functions in $\overset{\circ}{H}_j$ the inequality is well known and easily proved by using induction on j and performing an integration by parts (or by means of Fourier transforms). The Lemma is proved in the Appendix. Another proof, requiring slightly less regularity of the domain, was recently given by G. Ehrling [7].

<u>Definition</u>: (1) A domain $\mathcal{D}$ is said to have the cone property if every point in $\mathcal{D}$ is the vertex of a closed solid right spherical cone V of fixed opening and height which belongs to $\bar{\mathcal{D}}$.

(2) $\mathcal{D}$ is said to have the strong cone property if there exist positive constants d, λ and a cone V as above such that any points P, Q in $\bar{\mathcal{D}}$ with

$$s \equiv |P-Q| \leq d$$

are vertices of cones V_P, V_Q which are congruent to V, and have the property that the volume of the intersection of V_P, V_Q with $\bar{\mathcal{D}}$ and the two spheres with centers P, Q and radius s, is not less than λs^n.

It is easily seen that a domain of class C_2 satisfies the strong cone condition.

It is well known that a function in H_j, with a sufficiently large j, is continuous; we simply quote the following lemma of Sobolev [24], (see also Friedrichs [10]):

Lemma 7. _If u is in $H_{[n/2]+1}$ in a domain $\mathcal{D}$ having the cone property then u is continuous in $\bar{\mathcal{D}}$ and satisfies_

$$|u(x)| \leq \text{const. } |u|_{[n/2]+1}$$

where the constant depends only on the cone V.

Remark: Under the same hypothesis, if $\mathcal{D}$ has the strong cone property then we may assert that (i) for n odd, u satisfies a Hölder condition with exponent $\frac{1}{2}$, (ii) for n even, u satisfies a Hölder condition with any exponent < 1.

Lemma 8. _Let u be in $\mathring{H}_1$ in a domain $\mathcal{D}$ of class C_1. If_ u _is continuous in_ $\bar{\mathcal{D}}$ _then in fact_

$$u = 0 \quad \text{on } \dot{\mathcal{D}}.$$

Proof: Let P be a point on the boundary $\dot{\mathcal{D}}$, and consider u in a patch $\mathcal{A}$ of $\mathcal{D}$ near P. Since $\mathcal{D}$ is of class C_1 we may suppose (after a transformation of independent variable) that in a neighborhood of P the boundary of $\mathcal{A}$ lies in a hyperplane $x_n = 0$. Let S be an n dimensional right spherical cylinder with base on the hyperplane $x_n = 0$ and generators parallel to the x_n-axis. Assume that P is the center of the base and that the area of the base equals the height of the cylinder, which we denote by h. For a point x in S, and a continuously differentiable function u vanishing on $x_n = 0$, we have

$$u^2(x) = \left(\int_0^{x_n} u_{x_n} \, dx_n \right)^2 \leq h \int_0^{x_n} u_{x_n}^2 \, dx_n$$

so that, by integration over S,

$$(2.6) \qquad \int_S u^2 \, dx \leq h^2 \int_S u_{x_n}^2 \, dx \quad .$$

The given function u, being in $\mathring{H}_1$, can be approximated in the mean (together with its derivative) by such functions (together with their derivatives) so that (2.6) holds also for u. Writing the inequality in the form

$$(\text{Volume of } S)^{-1} \int_S u^2 dx \leq \int_S u_{x_n}^2 \, dx$$

we observe that as $h \to 0$ the left hand side converges to $u^2(P)$, by the continuity of u at P, while the right hand side tends to zero, since $S \to 0$. Thus $u(P) = 0$.

The following is easily verified.

Lemma 9. <u>Let $\mathcal{B}$ be a subdomain of $\mathcal{D}$ with $\bar{\mathcal{B}} \subset \mathcal{D}$. For a function u in H_j the difference quotient, say with respect to x_1,</u>

$$u^h = \frac{1}{h}(u(x_1 + h, x_2, \ldots, x_n) - u(x_1, x_2, \ldots, x_n))$$

<u>is well defined in $\mathcal{B}$ for h sufficiently small;</u> u^h <u>satisfies</u>

$$|u^h|_{j-1}^{\mathcal{B}} \leq |u^h|_j \quad \text{and} \quad \lim_{k \to 0} |u^h - u_{x_1}|_0^{\mathcal{B}} = 0 .$$

<u>In case u is in $\mathring{H}_j$ we may consider u extended to the whole space by making it vanish outside of $\mathcal{D}$. Then we have</u>

$$|u^h|_{j-1} \leq |u|_j \quad \text{and} \quad \lim_{k \to 0} |u^h - u_{x_1}|_0 = 0 .$$

3. The Existence Theory

We now give a brief description of the Hilbert space approach for the Dirichlet problem for equation (1.1)

$$Lu = f .$$

<u>Definition</u>. A function u which belongs to $H_0^{\mathcal{A}}$ for every compact subdomain $\mathcal{A}$ is said to be a weak solution if it satisfies the identity

$$(3.1) \qquad\qquad (L^* \phi, u) = (\phi, f)$$

for every test function ϕ. L^* is the formal adjoint of L. By integration by parts we see that any weak solution u having

continuous derivatives up to order 2m satisfies $(\phi, Lu) = (\phi, f)$ for every ϕ, and is therefore a solution in the classical sense.

The classical Dirichlet problem requires us to find a solution whose boundary values, and those of its derivatives up to order m-1, are given on the boundary. The Hilbert space information is by now classical:

The Generalized Dirichlet Problem. <u>Given functions u_0 in H_m, and f in H_0, find a weak solution u of the equation such that $u - u_0$ is in $\mathring{H}_m$; u is then considered to have the same Dirichlet data, in a generalized sense, as u_0.</u>

If u is such a solution, with L given by (1.1) we may, by partial integration, express (3.1) in the form

$$(3.2) \qquad B[\phi, u] \equiv \sum_{\rho, \sigma = 0}^{m} (D^\rho \phi, a^{\rho, \sigma} D^\sigma u) = (\phi, f) \ ,$$

or

$$(3.3) \qquad B[\phi, u - u_0] = (\phi, f) - B[\phi, u_0] \ .$$

We observe that $B[u, v]$ is linear in u, antilinear in v, and that, by Schwarz' inequality

$$(3.4) \qquad |B[u, v]| \leq \mathrm{const.} |u|_m \cdot |v|_m \ ,$$

the constant depending only on the bounds of the coefficients $a^{\rho, \sigma}$.

The existence theory applies to an operator which is uniformly elliptic, i.e. to one having bounded coefficients $a^{\rho, \sigma}$, and for which the characteristic polynomial is positive definite·

$$(3.5) \qquad \mathcal{R}e \, (-1)^m \xi^m a^{m,m} \xi^m \geq c_0 |\xi|^{2m} \ .$$

Here c_0 is a positive constant, $|\xi|$ denotes the length of the real vector ξ: $(\xi_1, \ldots, \xi_n)$, and ξ^m abbreviates any product of m of the $\xi_1, \ldots, \xi_n$.

We shall suppose the leading coefficients $a^{m,m}$ to be continuous in $\mathcal{E}$, and we shall use the letters c, k to

represent constants which depend only on c_0, the bounds on the coefficients $a^{\rho,\sigma}$, and on the modulus of continuity of the $a^{m,m}$.

Theorem 1. $\underline{\text{Let } L \text{ be uniformly elliptic.}}$ For k $\underline{\text{sufficiently large the generalized Dirichlet problem for the}}$ $\underline{\text{equation}}$

$$(L + k)u = f$$

$\underline{\text{admits a unique solution.}}$ For the equation $Lu = f$ $\underline{\text{we have the}}$ $\underline{\text{Fredholm alternative.}}$

The single estimate on which the proof of the theorem is based is

Gárding's Inequality [11]. $\underline{\text{For the uniformly elliptic}}$ $\underline{\text{operator } L \text{ there exist constants } c > 0 \underline{\text{ and }} k \underline{\text{ such that}}}$

$$(3.6) \qquad \mathcal{R}_e B[\phi,\phi] = \mathcal{R}_e(\phi, L\phi) \geq c|\phi|_m^2 - k|\phi|_0^2$$

$\underline{\text{holds for every test function}}\ \phi.$

Its derivation may be sketched as follows:

(i) In case L has only terms of order 2m with constant coefficients, (3.6) is proved with the aid of Fourier transforms. For variable coefficients the inequality is proved by (ii) breaking up the integrals, with the aid of partition of unity, into sums of integrals over small regions, (iii) approximating in each region the leading coefficients by their values at some point in the region and using the result already established in (i) for the constant coefficient case, and (iv) estimating the error term with the aid of Lemma 6 of §2 for the trivial case of functions in $\overset{\circ}{H}_m$.

Once (3.6) is established for functions with compact support it may be extended, by completion, to functions u in $\overset{\circ}{H}_m$:

$$(3.6)' \qquad \mathcal{R}_e B[u,u] \geq c|u|_m^2 - k|u|_0^2 \ .$$

In proving Theorem 1 we shall use a modified form of the projection theorem in Hilbert space. This is a generalized representation theorem for bounded linear functionals due to P. D. Lax and A. Milgram [18], which enables us to treat at once non-symmetric operators.

Representation Theorem.[3] Let $B[x,y]$ be a form defined
for pairs of elements x, y in a Hilbert space H (norm $|\ |$)
which is linear in x, antilinear in y, and satisfies

(3.4)' $$|B[x,y]| \leq \text{const.} |x| \cdot |y| .$$

Suppose that for some positive constant c

(3.7) $$|B[x,x]| \geq c|x|^2$$

for every x in H. Then every bounded linear functional $F(x)$
admits the representation

(3.8) $$F(x) = B[x,v] = \overline{B[w,x]} ,$$

for fixed elements v, w which are unique.

The principle feature to be noted is that no symmetry is
required of $B[x,y]$. The proof may be given in a few lines:
For any fixed v, $B[x,v]$ is a bounded linear functional of x and
therefore admits the representation

$$B[x,v] = (x,y)_H$$

for some element y, where on the right we have employed the
scalar product of H. This defines a mapping $y = Av$ which is
clearly linear. Letting $x = v$ and applying (3.7) we find that

$$c|v|^2 \leq |B[v,v]| \leq |(v,y)_H| \leq |v| \cdot |y| .$$
or
$$|v| \leq c^{-1}|y| .$$

It follows that the operator A has a bounded inverse and hence
that its range is closed. We see that the v corresponding to
any y is unique. To see that the range of A is the whole space
suppose that z is orthogonal to it. Then we have

$$B[z,v] = 0$$

for all v. But setting $v = z$ it follows from (3.7) that $z = 0$.
Thus A maps onto the whole space, and therefore every linear

functional $F(x)$, being of the form $(x,y)_H$ admits the representation $F(x) = B[x,v]$. The other representation is established in a similar way.

Before proving Theorem 1 we prove

Theorem 1'. <u>Let</u> $B[u,v]$ <u>be the bilinear form associated in (3.2) with the given form (1.1) of</u> L. <u>If there exists a positive constant</u> c <u>such that</u>

$$(3.7)' \qquad |B[\phi,\phi]| \geq c|\phi|_m^2$$

<u>for all test functions</u> ϕ, <u>then the generalized Dirichlet problem for</u> $Lu = f$ <u>admits a unique solution.</u>

Proof: From (3.4) and (3.7)', which by completion extends to functions in $\overset{\circ}{H}_m$, it follows that the form $B[u,v]$ satisfies in the Hilbert space $H = \overset{\circ}{H}_m$ all the hypotheses of the Representation Theorem, and we conclude that the bounded linear functional

$$F(\psi) = (\psi,f) - B[\psi,u_0] \ ,$$

defined for ψ in $\overset{\circ}{H}_m$, admits the representation $F(\psi) = B[\psi,v]$ for some (unique) function v in $\overset{\circ}{H}_m$. Setting $u = u_0 + v$ it follows that u satisfies (3.3) and is therefore the desired solution of the Dirichlet problem.

The first part of Theorem 1 now follows; for, in virtue of Gårding's inequality (3.6)' the operator $L + k$, to which is associated the form $B[u,v] + k(u,v)$, satisfies the hypotheses of Theorem 1'. To prove the second part we write the equation $Lu = f$ in the form $(L + k)u = ku + f$, or

$$u = k(L + k)^{-1}u + (L + k)^{-1}f \ .$$

Since by Gårding's inequality (3.6)', the operator $(L + k)^{-1}$ maps H_0 boundedly into $\overset{\circ}{H}_m$ it is completely continuous; by Rellich's lemma (see Courant-Hilbert [5], page 489), and from the Riesz theory of completely continuous operators we see that the alternative holds.

<u>Remark</u>: For the particular operator

$$(3.9) \qquad L_s = (-1)^s \triangle^s + 1$$

where $\triangle$ is the Laplacian the inequality

$$(\phi, L_0 \phi) \geq c |\phi|_s^2$$

clearly holds with some positive constant c for all test functions ϕ. This follows in fact by a direct partial integration, and with the aid of Lemma 6 of §2 in its trivial form -for functions with compact support.

A number of more general boundary value problems may be treated in a similar manner:[4] (For simplicity we consider only problems with homogeneous boundary data.) Let H be a closed subspace of H_m which contains $\mathring{H}_m$. H is then a Hilbert space with $| \ |_m$ as norm, and we formulate the problem: given f in H_0, find a function u in H such that

$$(3.2)' \qquad B[v,u] = (v,f) \ ,$$

for every function v in H. (Since only derivatives of u and v up to order m occur in $(3.2)'$ the equation is meaningful).

Consider, in particular, a second order elliptic operator in a smoothly bounded domain

$$L = - \frac{\partial}{\partial x_i} \left(a_{ij} \frac{\partial}{\partial x_j} \right) + a_i \frac{\partial}{\partial x_i} + a \ ,$$

with summation convention employed. Take $H = H_1$ and imagine a function u satisfying $(3.2)'$ and having continuous second derivatives in $\mathcal{D}$ and continuous first derivatives in the closure $\bar{\mathcal{D}}$. Then integration of $(3.2)'$ by parts shows that u satisfies the boundary condition $\xi_i a_{ij} u_j = 0$ where $(\xi_1, \ldots, \xi_n)$ is the normal vector on the boundary. The function u is thus a solution of the Neumann problem associated with the leading terms a_{ij}.

---

[4] This follows Gårding. For more general problems see Jacques-Louis Lions [19] and the papers referred to there, and F. E. Browder [2].

The existence theory presented here, for instance Theorem 1', may be extended to the more general problem (3.2)' provided that for some positive constant c we have

$$|B[u,u]| \geq c|u|_m^2 \text{ for all u in H.}$$

4. The Interior Differentiability of Weak Solutions

In this section we give a simple proof of the differentiability in the classical sense of weak solutions of equation (1.1).

In view of the result of Sobolev, Lemma 7 of §2, it suffices, in order to prove the continuity of a function and of its derivatives up to any order i, to prove the strong differentiability of the function (see §2) up to order $[n/2] + i + 1$, where n is the dimension. Therefore in this section we shall only be concerned with proving strong differentiability.

In the following the constants denoted simply by const. depend, as far as functions ϕ are concerned, only on the domain of support of ϕ.

Our aim is to prove the following theorems for operators L satisfying

$$|B[\phi,\phi]| \geq c|\phi|_m^2 - k|\phi|_0^2$$

for appropriate constants $c > 0$, k, and all test functions ϕ.

Theorem 1.[5] Let u be in H_0^2 in every compact subdomain $\mathcal{Q}$ of $\mathcal{B}$ and satisfy, for every test function ϕ and some j, $0 \leq j \leq 2m$, the inequality

$$(4.1) \qquad |(L^*\phi,u)| \leq \text{const.} |\phi|_{2m-j} .$$

If the coefficients $a^{\rho,\gamma}$ have continuous derivatives up to order m, then u has strong derivatives up to order j.

---

[5] The formulation of Theorem 1 and also the use of the inverse Laplacian (L_s^{-1}) employed in the proof were suggested by discussions with P. D. Lax.

Theorem 2. _Let u be in_ H_c^a _in every compact subdomain_ a _of_ $\mathcal{L}$ _and a weak solution of_ Lu = f. _If f has strong derivatives up to order_ p $\geq$ 0, _and the coefficients_ $a^{\rho,\nu}$ _possess continuous derivatives up to order_ max $(m,\rho+p)$, _then u has strong derivatives up to order_ 2m + p.

Within the framework of the L_2 theory Friedrichs [10] and Browder [1(d)] proved the differentiability of weak solutions which are already m times strongly differentiable. The proof of Theorem 1 is presented in a number of lemmas essentially contained in Friedrichs [10].

By our assumption on L we have

$$(4.2) \qquad |B[u,u]| \geq c|u|_m^2 - k|u|_0^2$$

valid, by completion, for all functions u in $\mathring{H}_m$.

Lemma 1. _Let u have strong derivatives of order m and satisfy_

$$(4.3) \qquad |B[\phi,u]| \leq \text{const.}|\phi|_{m-1} \ .$$

Suppose also that the coefficients $a^{\rho,\nu}$ _have continuous first derivatives, then u has strong derivatives of order_ m+1.

Proof: Let a, $\mathcal{B}$ and $\mathcal{C}$ be domains with $a \subset \bar{a} \subset \mathcal{B} \subset \bar{\mathcal{B}} \subset \mathcal{C} = \bar{\mathcal{C}} \subset \mathcal{D}$, where bar denotes closure, and let ζ be an infinitely differentiable positive function with support in $\mathcal{B}$ which is identically one in a and nowhere greater than one. Set $\zeta u = v$.

For h sufficiently small, and any point $P : (x_1,\ldots,x_n)$ in $\mathcal{B}$, the point $P_h : (x_1+h,x_2,\ldots,x_n)$ lies in $\mathcal{C}$. Denoting the difference quotient of a function g by

$$g^h = \frac{g(P_h) - g(P)}{h} \ ,$$

and regarding g^h as a function of P we find, using $K_1,K_2,\ldots$ to denote constants independent of ϕ, that

$$\left| B[\phi, v^h] \right| = \left| \sum_{\rho,\tau=0}^{m} (D^\rho \phi, a^{\rho,\tau} D^\sigma (\zeta u)^h \right|$$

$$\leq \left| \sum_{\rho,\tau=0}^{m} (D^\rho \phi, a^{\rho,\sigma} (\zeta D^\sigma u)^h \right| + K_1 |\phi|_m \cdot |u|_m^6 \, ,$$

where we have employed Lemma 9 of §2,

$$= \left| \sum_{\rho,\sigma=0}^{m} (D^\rho \phi, (a^{\rho,\sigma} \zeta D^\sigma u)^h - (a^{\rho,\sigma})^h \zeta(P_h) D^\sigma u(P_h) \right|$$

$$+ K_1 |\phi|_m \cdot |u|_m^6$$

$$\leq \left| \sum_{\rho,\sigma=0}^{m} (\zeta D^\rho \phi^{-h}, a^{\rho,\sigma} D^\sigma u) \right| + K_2 |\phi|_m \, ,$$

since the coefficients $a^{\rho,\sigma}$ have bounded first derivatives, and since $(f, g^h) = -(f^{-h}, g)$ if g vanishes in an h-strip near the boundary. Thus

$$\left| B[\phi, v^h] \right| \leq \left| \sum_{\rho,\sigma=0}^{m} (D^\rho(\zeta \phi^{-h}), a^{\rho,\sigma} D^\sigma u) \right| + K_3 |\phi^{-h}|_{m-1} + K_2 |\phi|_m$$

$$= \left| B[\zeta \phi^{-h}, u] \right| + K_3 |\phi^{-h}|_{m-1} + K_2 |\phi|_m \, .$$

Applying now (4.3) with ϕ replaced by $\zeta \phi^{-h}$ we infer that

$$\left| B[\phi, v^h] \right| \leq K_4 |\phi^{-h}|_{m-1} + K_2 |\phi|_m$$

(4.4)

$$\leq K_5 |\phi|_m$$

in virtue of Lemma 9 of §2. Since this inequality holds for all test functions ϕ it extends to all functions ϕ in H_m, and if we now set $\phi = v^h$ we find

$$\left| B[v^h, v^h] \right| \leq K_5 |v^h|_m \, .$$

Applying (4.2) we infer with the aid of Lemma 9 of §2 that

$$c\,|v^h|_m^2 \le K_5 |v^h|_m + k|v^h|_0^2$$

$$\le K_5 |v^h|_m + k|v|_1^2$$

from which it follows that $|v^h|_m$ is bounded by a constant independent of h.

Since now, by Lemma 9 of §2, v^h converges to $\partial v/\partial x_1$ in the mean, it follows from Lemma 1 of §2 that $\partial v/\partial x_1$ has strong derivatives of order m. Similarly, the other first derivatives of v may be shown to be m times strongly differentiable. By Lemma 2 of §2 it follows that v is (m+1) times strongly differentiable, and since $u \equiv v$ in $\mathcal{Q}$ it follows that u is in $H_{m+1}^{\mathcal{Q}}$, thus proving the lemma.

Lemma 2. <u>Let u have strong derivatives of order m</u> and <u>satisfy, for some integer j, $0 \le j \le m$,</u>

$$(4.5) \qquad |D[\phi,u]| \le \text{const.}\ |\phi|_{m-j}\ .$$

<u>If the coefficients $a^{\rho,\tau}$ have continuous derivatives up to order[6] max $(1,\rho-m+j)$ then u is (m+j) times strongly differentiable.</u>

Proof by induction: By Lemma 1 the lemma is true for $j = 1$. We shall prove it for any j supposing it to be true for $j-1$, $1 \le j-1 < m$; u is then (m+j-1) times strongly differentiable. Replacing ϕ in (4.5) by any derivative $D\phi$ of ϕ we have

$$(4.5)' \qquad |B[D\phi,u]| \le \text{const.}|D\phi|_{m-j} \le \text{const.}|\phi|_{m-j+1}\ .$$

By partial integration we easily see that

$$B[D\phi,u] = -\sum_{\rho,\tau=0}^{m} (D^\rho\phi, D(a^{\rho,\sigma} D^\sigma u))$$

$$= -B[\phi,Du] - \sum_{\rho,\tau} (D^\rho\phi, (Da^{\rho,\tau})\cdot D^\sigma u)\ .$$

---

[6] By modifying the proof we may slightly weaken the conditions on the coefficients.

Since u is (m+j-1) times strongly differentiable, and because
of the conditions on the coefficients, it follows, with the
aid of integration by parts, that

$$|B[\phi,Du]| \leq |B[D\phi,u]| + \text{const.}|\phi|_{m-j+1}$$
$$\leq \text{const.}|\phi|_{m-(j-1)}$$

in virtue of (4.5). But by the induction hypothesis the
function Du is then (m+j-1) times strongly differentiable, and
the conclusion follows by Lemma 2 of §2.

Lemma 3. <u>Let u be m times strongly differentiable and
be a weak solution of Lu = f, i.e. satisfy</u>

$$B[\phi,u] = (\phi,f) \quad \underline{\text{for all}}\ \phi$$

<u>If f is p times strongly differentiable and the coefficient</u>
$a^{\rho,\sigma}$ <u>are max $(1,\rho+p)$ times continuously differentiable then u
is (2m+p) times strongly differentiable.</u>

Proof: By Lemma 2 with j set equal to 2m, it follows
that u has strong derivatives up to order 2m. Thus Lemma 3
for p = 0 is proved. Suppose p = 1; we readily see that any
derivative Du of u is a weak solution of the differentiated
equation, or

$$B[\phi,Du] + (\phi,L'u) = (\phi,Df) \quad ,$$

where L' is the equation having as coefficients the D
derivatives of the coefficients of L. Therefore

$$|B[\phi,Du]| \leq \text{const.}|\phi|_0 \quad .$$

Applying Lemma 2 it follows that Du has strong derivatives of
order 2m. Since Du was any first derivative of u it follows
from Lemma 2 of §2 that u has strong derivatives of order 2m+1
For p > 1 this argument may be repeated.

Proof of Theorem 1: We may suppose that u is in L_2, by confining ourselves if necessary to a compact subdomain. The proof is by induction on j: assume the theorem true for all values $\leq$ j-1 < 2m; we wish to prove it for j. We can then say that u is (j-1) times strongly differentiable. If j-1 $\geq$ m the theorem follows from Lemma 2, and we therefore suppose that j-1 < m.

With the operator L_s as defined in (3.9) let h be the weak solution in $\overset{o}{H}_s$ of the equation

$$L_s h = u \quad \text{for} \quad s = m-j+1 .$$

By the existence theory of the previous section h exists. Since u is (j-1) times strongly differentiable it follows, by applying Lemma 3 to this equation, that h has strong derivatives up to order 2s+j-1 = m+s.

Substituting now for u in (4.1) we have

$$|(L\phi, L_s h)| \leq \text{const.} |\phi|_{2m-j} .$$

The expression on the left may be written in the form of (3.2),

$$(L\phi, L_s h) = B'[\phi, h] = \sum_{\alpha, \beta=0}^{m+s} (D^\alpha \phi, b^{\alpha,\beta} D^\beta h) ,$$

in which, from the conditions on the coefficients, one can see easily that the functions $b^{\alpha,\beta}$ possess continuous derivatives up to order max $(1, \alpha-m-s+j)$. Since furthermore the form B' is associated with the elliptic operator LL_s of order 2(m+s) we may apply Lemma 2 to the function h satisfying the inequality above,

$$|B'[\phi, h]| \leq \text{const.} |\phi|_{2m-j} = \text{const.} |\phi|_{m+s-1} ,$$

and conclude that h has strong derivatives up to order m+s+1. Since u is expressed in terms of the derivatives of h up to order 2s it follows that u has strong derivatives up to order m+s+1-2s = j, and the Theorem is proved.

Proof of Theorem 2: Theorem 2 follows immediately from Theorem 1 and Lemma 3.

It is clear that the arguments given here may be employed to derive estimates of the square integrals of derivatives of solutions of $Lu = f$. Such a priori estimates have been derived, for instance, by Friedrichs [10] with the aid of inequality (3.6), and since weak solutions have been shown to be strongly differentiable the estimates apply to them. A typical estimate for any compact subdomain $\mathcal{A}$ is

(i)

$$(4.6)_1 \qquad (|u|_m^{\mathcal{A}})^2 \le \text{const} \, (|u|_0^2 + |f|_0^2)$$

where the constant depends only on $\mathcal{A}$ and on bounds for the derivatives up to order m of the coefficients $a^{\rho,\tau}$,

(ii)

$$(4.6)_2 \qquad (|u|_j^{\mathcal{A}})^2 \le \text{const.} \, (|u|_0^2 + |f|_{j-2m}^2) \qquad \text{for} \quad j > 2m$$

where the constant depends only on $\mathcal{A}$ and on bounds for the derivative of the $a^{\rho,\sigma}$ up to order $\max \, (m, \rho+j-2m)$.

5. Differentiability at the Boundary

The solution $u \in H_m$ of the generalized Dirichlet problem (3.3) is a solution in the classical sense provided the boundary, the coefficients, and functions f and u_0 are sufficiently smooth. (See also the remark at the end of this section.) We shall prove this using Lemma 6 of §2 and arguments similar to those used in the proof of Lemmas 1-3 of §4.

To start, a few simplifying remarks:

(i) We assume first of all that $u_0 \equiv 0$, so that $u \in \mathring{H}_m$; for, if u_0 is sufficiently smooth it can simply be subtracted from u.

(ii) Once we have shown that u and its derivatives up to order $m-1$ are continuous in $\overline{\mathcal{B}}$ it follows from Lemma 8 of §2 that, in fact, they vanish on the boundary, so that the Dirichlet data is satisfied.

(iii) In order to prove that u has continuous derivatives of order i in $\overline{B}$ it suffices, in virtue of Lemma 7 of §2 (Sobolev) to show that u is in $H_{[n/2]+i-1}$. Thus we shall be concerned here only with proving that u is in H_{m+p} for any given $p > 0$. For this purpose we shall require that f be in H_{p-1}. We shall not keep a careful accounting of the differentiability requirements made on the coefficients of the equation or on the boundary. The reader can verify that it suffices that the $a^{\rho,\sigma}$ have continuous derivatives in $\overline{D}$ up to order max $(1,\rho+m+p-2)$ and that the domain belongs to class C_{3m+p-2}. These requirements are too restrictive; concerning f it should be sufficient, in analogy with Lemma 3, that f be in H_0 for $p \leq m$, and in H_{p-m} for $p > m$.[7] However our proof, based on Lemma 6' of §2 is too elementary to give the strong result except, of course, when $m = 1$ in which case the two requirements are the same. The case $m = 1$ has also been treated by O. Ladyzenskaia [16]. The appropriate a priori estimates for this case were also obtained by J. Schauder [22] in the plane and by R. Caccioppoli [3].

Thus under the results stated here on the coefficients and on the domain we prove the

Theorem. Let $u \in \overset{\circ}{H}_m$ be a solution of the generalized Dirichlet problem (3.3) ($u_0 = 0$). If f belongs to H_{p-1}, $p > 0$, then u belongs to H_{m+p}. In particular if $p = [n/2]+2$ then (by Theorem 2 of §4) u is 2m times continuously differentiable in $\overline{D}$ and (m+1) times continuously differentiable in $\overline{Fr}$, furthermore u and its derivatives up to order m-1 vanish on the boundary, so that u is a classical solution of the Dirichlet problem.

(iv) By Theorem 2, under the conditions on f and the the coefficient stated in (iii) the function u belongs to H^{B}_{2m+p-1} for every compact subdomain B. In virtue of Lemma 3 of §2 it therefore suffices to show that u is in H_{m+p} in a finite number of patches C near the boundary which, together with a compact subdomain B of D cover $\overline{D}$.

---

[7] This requirement suffices in Browder's proof, mentioned in the introduction.

(v) Consider any such patch G and a slightly larger patch Q containing it such that G is bounded away from that part of the boundary of $\mathcal{A}$ which does not belong to $\mathcal{B}$. By a transformation of coordinates in $\mathcal{A}$ we may assume that the part Q_1 of the boundary of $\mathcal{A}$ which belongs to $\mathcal{D}$ is planar and lies on $x_n = 0$. Denote the remainder of $\mathcal{A}$ by Q_2. Under the conditions in (iii) the coefficients $a^{\rho,\sigma}$ of the transformed equation in the new coordinates will continue to satisfy the requirements specified there, and u will belong to H_{2m+p-1} in any subdomain of $\mathcal{A}$ which is bounded away from $\mathcal{A}_1$.

(vi) We remark finally that, in virtue of Lemma 4 of §2, it suffices to prove that the derivatives of u up to order m+p are in H_0^G;

$$(5.1) \qquad D^j u \in H_0^G , \qquad\qquad j \leq m+p .$$

This we now proceed to show. In the patch $\mathcal{A}$ with part of its boundary on $x_n = 0$ all derivatives of u up to order m are in $H_0^{\mathcal{A}}$. Let us rename the coordinates and denote $(x_1,\ldots,x_{n-1})$ by x, and x_n by y. I claim that by the arguments used in proving Lemmas 1-3 of §4 we may show that all tangential (to $\mathcal{A}_1$) derivatives, $D_x^i u$, for $i \leq m+p-1$, have finite norm:

$$|D_x^i u|_m^G ,$$

where D_x^i denotes any derivative of order i involving only the variables x: $(x_1,\ldots,x_{n-1})$, in other words that all derivatives of the form

$$(5.2) \qquad D_x^i D^j u , \qquad i \leq m+p-1 , \qquad j \leq m ,$$

are in L_2 in G, i.e. in H_0^G. To verify first that $|D_x u|_m^G$ is finite--that is the analogue of Lemma 1 of §4--we introduce a cut off function ζ which is identically one in G and vanishes near $\mathcal{A}_2$, and apply a difference quotient operation in a <u>tangential direction</u>, as in the proof of Lemma 1. Since, in G, u is the limit under the norm $| \ |_m^G$ of functions vanishing

near α_1 the same is true for the difference quotients of u in tangential directions. Thus following the proof of Lemma 1, we find $|D_x u|_m^{\mathcal{C}}$ is finite, and it therefore follows also that any tangential derivative $D_x u$ is the limit, under $|\ |_m^{\mathcal{C}}$, of functions vanishing near α_1. To show that higher order tangential derivatives have finite norm $|\ |_m^{\mathcal{C}}$ we merely differentiate the equation repeatedly in tangential directions and apply the result just obtained to the differentiated equations--just as in the proofs of Lemma 2 and 3 of §4. In this manner we find that all derivatives of the form (5.2) belong to $H_0^{\mathcal{C}}$

In case $m = 1$ we are essentially through: Consider first $p = 1$; the only second derivative which we have not shown to be in $H_0^{\mathcal{C}}$ is $D_y^2 u$. But from the equation $Lu = f$ this term may be expressed in terms of f and the other derivatives of u; it therefore follows that it is also in $H_0^{\mathcal{C}}$. In case $p = 2$ we apply this same argument to the equation differentiated once in a tangential direction, $D_x Lu = D_x f$, and conclude, from the fact that the derivatives of the form $D_x^i D^j u$, with $i \leq 2$, $j \leq 1$, are in $H_0^{\mathcal{C}}$, that also $D_y^2 D_x u$ is in $H_0^{\mathcal{C}}$. Applying now D_y to the equation we see that $D_y^3 u$ is given in terms of $D_y f$ and other derivatives of u which we already know to be in $H_0^{\mathcal{C}}$. Thus also $D_y^3 u$, and hence any third order derivative $D^3 u$, is in $H_0^{\mathcal{C}}$, and the assertion (5.1) is proved. Repeating this argument we may establish (5.1) for any $p > 0$, in case $m = 1$.

Suppose now, however, that $m > 1$, and consider again the case $p = 1$. We know that all derivatives of the form (5.2)

$$(5.2)' \qquad\qquad D_x^i D^j u\ , \qquad\qquad i \leq m\ ,\quad j \leq m\ ,$$

are in $H_0^{\mathcal{C}}$. This includes all derivatives of order $m+1$ except $D_y^{m+1} u$. For $m > 1$ the equation $Lu = f$ no longer enables us to express this derivative in terms of others which are known to be in $H_0^{\mathcal{C}}$. Nevertheless the idea involved in the proof for the case $m = 1$ can be extended. The terms in Lu which are not

known, at this point, to be in H_0^ℓ are all those involving
derivatives of order $\leq 2m$ which are not of the form (5.2)',
i.e. the terms of the form

$$(5.3) \qquad (\text{coeff.}) \cdot D_y^{m+1} D^j u \ , \qquad\qquad j \leq m-1 \ .$$

The sum of terms of this form can therefore be written in the
form

$$D_y^m (\text{Some linear combination of } D^j u \text{ for } j \leq m) \equiv D_y^m g \ .$$

Because of the ellipticity of the equation we observe that the
coefficient, a_0, of $D_y^m u$ in g is bounded away from zero.

Thus we have the situation that the function g, together
with its derivative $(D_y^m g)$ belongs to H_0^ℓ. Here we can apply
Lemma 6 of §2, and we conclude that

$$(5.4) \qquad D_y^i g \in H_0^\ell \quad \text{for} \quad i \leq m \ .$$

In particular $D_y g \in H_0^\ell$. Differentiating out the expression
for g we see that the only term occurring in $D_y g$ which is not
already known to be in H_0^ℓ is $(a_0 D_y^{m-1} u)$. Since, by the remark
above, a_0 is bounded away from zero it follows that $D_y^{m+1} u$ is
in H_0^ℓ, and (5.1) is proved for $p = 1$.

In case $p = 2$ we know, to begin with, that derivatives
of the form (5.2).

$$(5.2)'' \qquad D_x^i D^j u \ , \qquad\qquad i \leq m+1 \ , \quad j \leq m$$

belong to H_0^ℓ. We do not obtain the desired result by simply
setting $i = 2$ in (5.4); for, $D_y^2 g$ contains many terms not as yet
known to be in H_0^ℓ. First, applying the argument just given for
$p = 1$ to the differentiated equation $D_x L u = D_x f$, we conclude
that derivatives of the form $D_y^{m+1} D_x u$ are in H_0^ℓ. Returning to
$D_y^2 g$ we now find that the only term not as yet in H_0^ℓ is $a_0 D_y^{m+2} u$
and it therefore follows that also $D_y^{m+2} u$, hence every
derivative $D^{m+2} u$, is in H_0^ℓ.

For $p = 3, 4, \ldots, p \leq m$, we successively repeat this
argument, first differentiating the equation in tangential
directions and then applying (5.4) for $i = p$. In case $p > m$

we no longer apply (5.4). For p = m+1, for instance, we
continue to differentiate the equation in tangential directions
and show that all derivatives of order 2m+1 except $D_y^{2m+1}u$ are
in H_0^{ζ}. $D_y^{2m+1}u$ is seen to be in H_0^{ζ} by consideration of
$D_yLu = D_y f$. One repeats this procedure for higher p.

This completes the proof of (5.1).

We observe that, analogous to the interior estimate (4.6)
we may establish the inequality

$$|u|_{m+p}^2 \leq \text{const.} \, (|u|_0^2 + |f|_{p-1}^2) \quad ,$$

with the constant depending only on the coefficients and on
the domain. As remarked earlier the condition on f is too
restrictive.

Remark: What about the smoothness up to the boundary of
solutions of other than the Dirichlet problem? It is clear
that the argument given here can be extended to a wide variety
of other problems. In particular consider the generalized
problem formulated on page 17. If, after transformation to a
patch with partly planar boundary, a shift along the boundary
of functions in the Hilbert space H and multiplication by a
suitable cut off function ζ does not take the functions out of
H the proof given here carries over in its present form
(provided (4.2) holds for functions in H). This will certainly
be the case if $H = H_m$, i.e. for the Neumann problem associated
with the bilinear form $B[v,u]$. Thus we have the

Theorem. Let $u \in H_m$ be a solution of the Neumann problem
(3.2)' associated with the bilinear form $B[v,u]$. If f belongs
to H_{p-1}, p > 0, then u belongs to H_{m+p}. In particular, if
p = [n/2] + 2 then u is 2m times continuously differentiable in
$\mathcal{D}$ and m+1 times continuously differentiable in $\bar{\mathcal{D}}$. Furthermore, u satisfies the boundary conditions appropriate to the
problem.

30

6. Strongly Elliptic Systems

Consider a system of differential equations with complex coefficients

$$(6.1) \qquad \ell_{ij}(x,D)u_j = f_i \ , \qquad\qquad i = 1,\ldots,N \ ,$$

(using summation convention) in functions $U: (u_1,\ldots,u_N)$. For $f = (f_1,\ldots,f_N)$ this may be expressed in the form

$$(6.1)' \qquad\qquad LU = f \ ;$$

$\ell_{ij}(x,D)$ is a differential operator, i.e. a polynomial in $D: (D_{x_1},\ldots,D_{x_n})$, with variable coefficients. Assume that there are non-negative integers $s_1,\ldots,s_N$ such that the order of ℓ_{ij} is not greater than $s_i + s_j$. Denoting by $\ell_{ij}'(x,D)$ the sum of terms in ℓ_{ij} of order exactly $s_i + s_j$, we define the characteristic matrix, involving a real vector $\zeta: (\zeta_1,\ldots,\zeta_n)$, as

$$\ell_{ij}'(x,\xi) \ .$$

The system is called elliptic if there exist appropriate $s_1,\ldots,s_N$ such that at every point in the domain

$$\det (\, \ell_{ij}'(x,\xi)) \neq 0 \quad \text{when} \quad \xi \neq 0 \ .$$

This definition is a special case of a more general definition of ellipticity given in [6].

Strong Ellipticity: The system (6.1) is called strongly elliptic if there exist appropriate $s_1,\ldots,s_N$ such that the quadratic form associated with the characteristic matrix is definite, i.e. if at every point in $\mathcal{D}$ and for a real vector $\xi: (\xi_1,\ldots,\xi_n)$ and a complex vector $\eta: (\eta_1,\ldots,\eta_n)$,

$$\ell_{ij}'(x,\xi)\eta_i \bar{\eta}_j \neq 0 \quad \text{when} \quad \xi \neq 0 \ , \quad \eta \neq 0 \ .$$

This definition of strong ellipticity reduces to that of Vishik [26] in case the s_i are equal. We shall assume that the s_i are

positive; otherwise the functions u_i corresponding to those i
for which $s_i = 0$ may be expressed explicitly in terms of the
other functions, see Remark 1 in §1 of [6].

Consider a system (6.1) with ℓ_{ij} given in the form

$$(6.2) \qquad \ell_{ij} = \sum_{\rho=0}^{s_i} \sum_{\sigma=0}^{s_j} (-1)^\rho D^\rho a_{ij}^{\rho,\sigma} D^\sigma$$

where summation is first extended over all derivatives D^ρ, D^σ
of orders ρ and σ; assume that the system is uniformly
strongly elliptic, i.e. that the coefficients $a_{ij}^{\rho,\sigma}$ are uniformly bounded, and that for some positive constant c_0 the
inequality

$$(6.3) \qquad \mathrm{Re}\ \xi^{s_i} a_{ij}^{s_i,s_j} \zeta^{s_j} \eta_i \bar{\eta}_j \geq c_0 \sum_i |\eta_i|^2 |\xi|^{2s_i}$$

holds, where $|\zeta|^2 = \sum \xi_i^2$; and of course there is summation
implied on the left.

The Dirichlet problem corresponding to (6.1) is: find a
solution $U\colon (u_1,\ldots,u_N)$ with u_i and its derivatives up to
order s_i-1 prescribed on the boundary, i.e.

$$u_i,\ \frac{\partial u_i}{\partial n},\ \ldots,\ \frac{\partial^{s_i-1} u_i}{\partial n^{s_i-1}}, \qquad\qquad i = 1,\ldots,N$$

given on the boundary, where $\partial/\partial n$ denotes differentiation in
the normal direction.

Thus as far as the Dirichlet problem is concerned the
system behaves as though it were of order $2s_i$ in u_i --despite
the fact that higher order derivatives of u_i may occur, as in
the example in the introduction.

Generalized Dirichlet problem: The Hilbert space formulation of the problem is as follows· given $f_1,\ldots,f_N$ in H_0 and
functions $U^{(0)}\colon (u_1^{(0)},\ldots,u_N^{(0)})$, with $u_i^{(0)}$ in H_{s_i}, find a weak
solution U of (6.1) i.e. U in H_0 satisfying

$$(6.1)' \qquad\qquad (L^*\Phi,U) = (\Phi,f)$$

for test vectors $\bar{\Phi}$: $(\phi_1,\ldots,\phi_n)$, and such that $(u_i - u_i^{(0)})$ is in $\mathring{H}_{s_i}$, $i = 1,\ldots,N$.

The existence theory of §3 for the Dirichlet problem extends immediately to our system. In particular Gårding's inequality is easily extended.

Gårding's Inequality. <u>There exist constants</u> c, k <u>depending only on</u> c_0, <u>the bounds on the coefficients</u> $a_{ij}^{\rho,\tau}$, <u>and on the modulus of continuity of the leading coefficients</u> $a_{ij}^{s_i,s_j}$, <u>such that</u>

$$(6.4) \qquad \mathrm{Re}\ (\bar{\Phi}.L\bar{\Phi}) \geq c \sum_i |\phi_i|_{s_i}^2 - k \sum_i |\phi_i|_0^2$$

<u>for every</u> $\bar{\Phi}$: $(\phi_1,\ldots,\phi_N)$.

The proof of the inequality (6.4) for the case of a single equation, as given for instance in [11], carries over immediately to the system. We shall describe here the first step of the proof that treats an operator L having constant coefficients $a_{ij}^{\rho,\tau}$ which, except for the highest order coefficients $a_{ij}^{s_i,s_j}$, are all zero. In this case, assuming (6.3), we have, in fact,

$$(6.5) \qquad \mathrm{Re}\ (\bar{\Phi},L\bar{\Phi}) \geq c_0 \sum_i \int |D^{s_i}\phi_i|^2 dx$$

where on the right we first sum over all derivatives D^{s_i} of order s_i. (6.5) is proved with the aid of the Fourier transform. Introducing the Fourier transform of any ϕ

$$\tilde{\phi} = \int e^{ix\xi}\phi(x)dx$$

we observe that $\widetilde{D^j\phi} = (-i)^j \xi^j \tilde{\phi}$ and that, from Parseval's formula,

$$\mathrm{Re}\,(L\Phi,\Phi) = (2\pi)^{-n}\,\mathrm{Re}\int (-1)^{s_j}(-1)^{s_j+s_k}\xi^{s_j}a_{jk}^{s_j,\,s_k}\xi^{s_k}\tilde{\phi}_j\bar{\phi}_k\,d\xi$$

$$= (2\pi)^{-n}\,\mathrm{Re}\int \xi^{s_j}a_{jk}^{s_j,\,s_k}\xi^{s_k}(i^{s_j}\tilde{\phi}_j)\cdot\overline{(i^{s_k}\tilde{\phi}_k)}\,d\xi =$$

$$\geq (2\pi)^{-n}c_0\int \sum_j |\tilde{\phi}_j|^2|\xi|^{2s_j}\,d\xi$$

by (6.3),

$$= c_0 \sum_j |D^{s_j}\phi_j|^2\,dx \quad.$$

The derivation of (6.4) for equations with variable coefficients is then carried out in the manner sketched in §3 (see [11]).

Concerning the differentiability of solutions, all considerations of §4 and §5 for a single elliptic equation extend to our elliptic system satisfying

$$(6.4)'\qquad |(\Phi,L\Phi)| \geq c \sum_i |\phi_i|^2_{s_i} - k \sum_i |\phi_i|^2_0$$

for appropriate constants $c > 0$, k, and all test functions $\Phi\colon (\phi_1,\ldots,\phi_N)$. For strongly elliptic systems of second order (i.e. $s_i = 1$) the smoothness of solutions up to the boundary has been demonstrated by C. B. Morrey [20]).

Summarizing, we state the

Theorem. (1) Let L be uniformly strongly elliptic in D (satisfying (6.3)), with leading coefficients $a_{ij}^{s_i,\,s_j}$ continuous in $\bar{D}$. Then for some constant k the generalized Dirichlet problem for the equation $(L + kI)U = f$, I the identity operator, admits a unique solution, while the alternative holds for the operator $LU = f$. (2) Suppose that L has sufficiently differentiable coefficients and that f has sufficiently many strong derivatives. If L satisfies (6.4)' then every weak solution U of (6.1)' is a classical solution of (6.1). If, in addition, U is a solution of the generalized Dirichlet problem, with f and $U^{(0)}$ sufficiently differentiable, then U is a solution of the problem in the classical sense.

34

Appendix: Proof of Lemma 6

The inequality (2.5) is a consequence of the following fact:

For sufficiently small ϵ there exists a constant $c(j)$ depending only on j and $\mathcal{D}$ such that for all u in H_j in $\mathcal{D}$ of class C_2

$$(1) \qquad \int_{\mathcal{D}} |D^i u|^2 dx \leq \epsilon \int_{\mathcal{D}} |D^j u|^2 dx + \epsilon^{-i/(j-i)} c(j) \int_{\mathcal{D}} |u|^2 dx \ , \quad i < j \ ,$$

where, on the right summation is extended over all derivatives of order j. It suffices to prove (1) for functions with continuous derivatives up to order j. Although our proof of (1) requires slightly more regularity of the domain than the proof given by G. Ehrling [7], it may be clearly generalized to yield the inequality for $p \geq 1$: for sufficiently small ϵ,

$$(1)' \qquad \int_{\mathcal{D}} |D^i u|^p dx \leq \epsilon \int_{\mathcal{D}} |D^j u|^p dx + c \int_{\mathcal{D}} |u|^p dx \ , \quad \text{for} \ i < j \ ,$$

where c is a constant depending only on ϵ, j, p and $\mathcal{D}$.

Our proof of (1) is based on an analogous estimate for functions of one variable which is essentially equivalent to inequality 259 in Hardy, Littlewood and Polya [13]. The one dimensional analogue of (1)' was proved earlier by I. Halpern and H. R. Pitt [12].

Consider first a function $u(x)$ defined in a (possibly infinite) interval $\mathcal{D}$. For $\epsilon \leq 4$ (length of $\mathcal{D}$)^2 we shall establish the inequality

$$(2) \qquad \int |Du|^2 dx \leq \epsilon \int |D^2 u|^2 dx + \frac{2^9}{\epsilon} \int |u|^2 dx \ .$$

To this end imagine the interval $\mathcal{D}$ divided into a number of subintervals such that the length of each is bounded by

$$(3) \qquad \frac{1}{4} \epsilon \leq \text{length}^2 \leq \frac{1}{2} \epsilon \ .$$

Let $a_1 \leq x \leq b_1$ be such a subinterval; divide it into three successive intervals of lengths a, $2a$ and a, so that $b_1 - a_1 = 4a$.

35

If x_1 and x_2 are points in the first and third intervals we have by the theorem of the mean,

$$Du \text{ (at some point)} = \frac{u(x_2) - u(x_1)}{x_2 - x_1}$$

so that

$$|Du(x)| \leq \frac{|u(x_2)| + |u(x_1)|}{2a} + \int_{a_1}^{b_1} |D^2u|\,dx \quad .$$

Now integrating with respect to x_1 and x_2 separately over the first and third intervals we find

$$a^2|Du| \leq \frac{1}{2} \int_{a_1}^{b_1} |u|\,dx + a^2 \int_{a_1}^{b_1} |D^2u|\,dx$$

and, dividing by a^2 and squaring

$$|Du|^2 \leq \frac{2}{4a^4} \left(\int_{a_1}^{b_1} |u|\,dx \right)^2 + 2 \left(\int_{a_1}^{b_1} |D^2u|\,dx \right)^2$$

$$\leq \frac{2}{a^3} \int |u|^2\,dx + 8a \int |D^2u|^2\,dx$$

by Schwarz' inequality. Integrating finally with respect to x we obtain the inequality

$$\int_{a_1}^{b_1} |Du|^2\,dx \leq \frac{8}{a^2} \int |u|^2\,dx + 32a^2 \int |D^2u|^2\,dx$$

$$= 2(b_1 - a_1)^2 \int |D^2u|^2\,dx + \frac{2^7}{(b_1 - a_1)^2} \int |u|^2\,dx$$

$$\leq \epsilon \int_{a_1}^{b_1} |D^2u|^2\,dx + \frac{2^9}{\epsilon} \int_{a_1}^{b_1} |u|^2\,dx \quad \text{by (3)} .$$

Summation over all the subintervals yields the desired result (2).

36

Consider now functions $u(x_1,\ldots,x_n)$ in the domain $\mathcal{D}$. Since $\mathcal{D}$ is of class C_2 one easily sees that $\mathcal{D}$ may be covered by a compact subdomain $\mathcal{B}$ and patches such that the closure of each patch may be mapped in a one-to-one way onto a cube by a mapping which, together with its inverse, is twice continuously differentiable. In each such cube we may apply inequality (2) on line segments parallel to the edges. Integrating with respect to the orthogonal directions we obtain the inequality

$$\int |Du|^2 dx \leq \epsilon \int |D^2 u|^2 dx + 2^9 \epsilon^{-1} \int |u|^2 dx$$

for sufficiently small ϵ. Here summation over all first and second derivatives is implied. An analogous inequality therefore holds in the patch, and also in $\mathcal{B}$, since also $\mathcal{B}$ may be covered by a finite number of cubes. Summing over these cubes and patches, we find for ϵ sufficiently small, and some constant $c > 1$ depending only on $\mathcal{D}$, that

$$(2)' \qquad \int_{\mathcal{D}} |Du|^2 dx \leq \epsilon \int_{\mathcal{D}} |D^2 u|^2 + \frac{c}{\epsilon} \int_{\mathcal{D}} |u|^2 dx \quad .$$

To derive the general result (1) we use induction on j. For $j = 1$ the inequality obviously holds. Suppose it is true for $j \leq k$ and we wish to verify it for $j = k+1$. Consider first $i = k$. Applying (2)' to the function $D^{k-1}u$, with ϵ replaced by $\epsilon/2$, we find

$$\int |D^k u|^2 dx \leq \frac{\epsilon}{2} \int |D^{k+1} u|^2 + 2c\epsilon^{-1} \int |D^{k-1} u|^2 dx \quad .$$

By induction hypothesis, however, for any small $\delta > 0$

$$\int |D^{k-1} u|^2 dx \leq \delta \int |D^k u|^2 dx + \delta^{-(k-1)} c(k) \int |u|^2 dx \quad .$$

Choosing $\delta = \epsilon(4c)^{-1}$ and inserting into the above inequality we find

$$\int |D^k u|^2 dx \leq \epsilon \int |D^{k+1} u|^2 dx + \epsilon^{-k} c'(k) \int |u|^2 dx$$

which has the desired form. For $i < k$ we have

$$\int |D^i u|^2 dx \leq \delta \int |D^k u|^2 dx + \delta^{-i/(k-i)} c(k) \int |u|^2 dx \quad ,$$

by induction,

$$\leq \delta\mu \int |D^{k+1} u|^2 dx + \delta\mu^{-k} c'(k) \int |u|^2 dx + \delta^{-i/(k-i)} c(k) \int |u|^2 dx$$

by the result just obtained. Setting $\delta = \varepsilon^{(k-i)/(k+1-i)}$, $\mu = \varepsilon^{1/(k+1-i)}$ yields the inequality (1) for ε sufficiently small.

Bibliography

[1] Browder, F. E., (a) The Dirichlet problem for linear
    elliptic equations of arbitrary even order with variable
    coefficients, Proc. Nat. Acad. Sci. U.S.A., Vol. 38,
    1952, pp. 230-235.
    (b) The Dirichlet and vibrations problems for linear
    elliptic differential equations of arbitrary order, Proc.
    Nat. Acad. Sci. U.S.A., Vol. 38, 1952, pp. 741-747.
    (c) Assumption of boundary values and the Green's function
    in the Dirichlet problem for the general elliptic
    equation, Proc. Nat. Acad. Sci. U.S.A., Vol. 39, 1953,
    pp. 179-184.
    (d) Strongly elliptic systems of differential equations,
    Contributions to the Theory of Partial Differential
    Equations, Ann. Math. Studies No. 33, Princeton, 1954,
    pp. 15-51.

[2] Browder, F. E., Linear parabolic differential equations of
    arbitrary order; general boundary-value problems for
    elliptic equations, Proc. Nat. Acad. Sci. U.S.A., Vol. 39,
    1953, pp. 185-190.

[3] Caccioppoli, R., Limitazioni integrali per le soluzioni di
    un'equazione lineare ellittica a derivate parziali,
    Giorn. Mat. Battaglini, Vol. 80, 1950-51, pp. 186-212.

[4] Calderon, A. P., and Zygmund, A., On the existence of
    singular integrals, Acta. Math., Vol. 88, 1952, pp. 85-139.

[5] Courant, R. and Hilbert, D., Methoden der mathematischen
    Physik, Vol. 2, Chap. 7, Springer, Berlin, 1937.

[6] Douglis, A. and Nirenberg, L., Interior estimates for
    elliptic systems of partial differential equations, Comm.
    Pure and Appl. Math., this issue.

[7] Ehrling, G., On a type of eigenvalue problems for certain
    elliptic differential operators, Math. Scandinavica,
    Vol. 2, 1954, pp. 267-285.

38

[8] Friedrichs, K. O., On differential operators in Hilbert
     spaces, Amer. J. Math., Vol. 61, No. 2, 1939,
     pp. 523-544.

[9] Friedrichs, K. O., The identity of weak and strong
     extensions of differential operators, Trans. Amer. Math.
     Soc., Vol. 55, No. 1, 1944, pp. 132-151.

[10] Friedrichs, K. O., On the differentiability of the
     solutions of linear elliptic differential equations,
     Comm. Pure and Appl. Math., Vol. 6, 1953, pp. 299-326.

[11] Gårding, L., Dirichlet's problem for linear elliptic
     partial differential equations, Math, Scandinavica,
     Vol. 1, 1953, pp. 55-72.

[12] Halpern, I. and Pitt, H. R., Integral inequalities
     connected with differential operators, Duke Math. J.,
     Vol. 4, 1938, pp. 613-625.

[13] Hardy, G. H., Littlewood, J. E., and Polya, G.,
     Inequalities, The University Press, Cambridge, 1934.

[14] John, F., (a) The fundamental solution of linear elliptic
     differential equations with analytic coefficients, Comm.
     Pure and Appl. Math., Vol. 3, 1950, pp. 273-304.
     (b) General properties of solutions of linear elliptic
     partial differential equations, Proc. Symp. Spectral
     Theory and Differential Problems, Oklahoma College,
     1951, pp. 113-175.

[15] John, F., Derivatives of continuous weak solutions of
     linear elliptic equations, Comm. Pure and Appl. Math.,
     Vol. 6, 1953, pp. 327-335.

[16] Ladyzenskaia, O., On the closure of an elliptic operator,
     Doklady Akad. Nauk SSSR, Vol. 79, 1951, pp. 723-725.

[17] Lax, P. D., On Cauchy's problem for hyperbolic equations
     and the differentiability of solutions of elliptic
     equations, Comm. Pure and Appl. Math., this issue.

[18] Lax, P. D., and Milgram, A., Parabolic equations,
     Contributions to the Theory of Partial Differential
     Equations, Ann. Math. Studies No. 33, Princeton, 1954,
     pp. 167-190.

[19] Lions, J. L., Sur les problèmes de dérivées oblique,
     C. R. Acad. Sci. Paris, Vol. 240, January 1955,
     pp. 266-268.

[20] Morrey, C. B., Second order elliptic systems of
     differential equations, Contributions to the Theory of
     Partial Differential Equations, Ann. Math. Studies
     No. 33, Princeton, 1954, pp. 101-159.

[21] Riesz, F. and Nagy, B. Sz., Leçons d'Analyse Fonctionelle,
     Akadémiai Kiadó, Budapest, 1952.

39

[22] Schauder, J., Sur les équations linéaires du type
     elliptique à coefficients continus, C. R. Acad. Sci.
     Paris, Vol. 199, 1934, pp. 1366-1368.

[23] Schwartz, L., Théorie des Distributions I, Hermann,
     Paris 1950.

[24] Sobolev, On a theorem of functional analysis, Mat.
     Sbornik, N.S. 4, 1938, pp. 471-497.

[25] Van Hove, L., Sur l'extension de la condition de Legendre
     du calcul des variations aux intégrales multiples à
     plusieurs fonctions inconnues, Indagationes Math.,
     Vol. 7, 1, 1947, pp. 3-8.

[26] Vishik, M. I., (a) The method of orthogonal and direct
     decomposition in the theory of elliptic partial
     differential equations. Mat. Sbornik, Vol. 25, 1949
     pp. 189-234.
     (b) On Strongly elliptic systems of differential
     equations, Mat. Sbornik, Vol. 29, 1951, pp. 617-676.

[27] Weyl, H., The method of orthogonal projection in potential
     theory, Duke Math. J., Vol. 7. 1940, pp. 411-444.